The boat ride

Rigby®

A Harcourt Achieve Imprint

www.Rigby.com
1-800-531-5015

Here comes Monkey.

Monkey is in the boat.

Here comes Rabbit.

Rabbit is in the boat.

Here comes Little Teddy.

Little Teddy is not in the boat.

Here comes the boat.

Little Teddy

is in the boat, too.